ANIMAL SAFARI

Tigers

by Derek Zobel

BLASTOFF! READERS

BELLWETHER MEDIA · MINNEAPOLIS, MN

Note to Librarians, Teachers, and Parents:

Blastoff! Readers are carefully developed by literacy experts and combine standards-based content with developmentally appropriate text.

Level 1 provides the most support through repetition of high-frequency words, light text, predictable sentence patterns, and strong visual support.

Level 2 offers early readers a bit more challenge through varied simple sentences, increased text load, and less repetition of high-frequency words.

Level 3 advances early-fluent readers toward fluency through increased text and concept load, less reliance on visuals, longer sentences, and more literary language.

Level 4 builds reading stamina by providing more text per page, increased use of punctuation, greater variation in sentence patterns, and increasingly challenging vocabulary.

Level 5 encourages children to move from "learning to read" to "reading to learn" by providing even more text, varied writing styles, and less familiar topics.

Whichever book is right for your reader, Blastoff! Readers are the perfect books to build confidence and encourage a love of reading that will last a lifetime!

This edition first published in 2012 by Bellwether Media, Inc.

No part of this publication may be reproduced in whole or in part without written permission of the publisher. For information regarding permission, write to Bellwether Media, Inc., Attention: Permissions Department, 5357 Penn Avenue South, Minneapolis, MN 55419.

Library of Congress Cataloging-in-Publication Data

Zobel, Derek, 1983-
Tigers / by Derek Zobel.
    p. cm. – (Blastoff! Readers. Animal safari)
Includes bibliographical references and index.
Summary: "Developed by literacy experts for students in kindergarten through grade three, this book introduces tigers to young readers through leveled text and related photos"–Provided by publisher.
ISBN 978-1-60014-610-7 (hardcover : alk. paper)
1. Tiger–Juvenile literature. I. Title.
QL737.C23Z637 2011
599.756–dc22   2011005611

Printed in the United States of America, North Mankato, MN.

080111   1187

Contents

What Are Tigers?

Tigers are the largest **wild** cats in the world.

They roam forests, grasslands, and swamps. Most tigers live alone.

Tigers spend a lot of time near water. Sometimes they go for a swim!

Tiger Stripes

All tigers have dark stripes. Each tiger has more than 100 stripes.

Hunting

Tigers **stalk** boars, deer, and other **prey**. They move slowly when they stalk.

Tigers stay low to the ground until they are close to prey. Then they **pounce**!

Cubs

Female tigers give birth to **cubs**. The cubs live in a **den** for six months.

Cubs can hunt prey when they are one year old.

This young tiger caught a deer. Dinner time!

Glossary

cubs—young tigers

den—a cave or hole where some animals give birth and live

pounce—to leap on top of something

prey—animals that are hunted by other animals for food

stalk—to secretly follow

wild—living in nature

To Learn More

AT THE LIBRARY

Hewett, Joan. *A Tiger Cub Grows Up.* Minneapolis, Minn.: Carolrhoda Books, 2002.

Kalman, Bobbie. *Endangered Tigers.* New York, N.Y.: Crabtree Pub., 2004.

Squire, Ann. *Tigers.* New York, N.Y.: Children's Press, 2005.

ON THE WEB

Learning more about tigers is as easy as 1, 2, 3.

1. Go to www.factsurfer.com.

2. Enter "tigers" into the search box.

3. Click the "Surf" button and you will see a list of related Web sites.

With factsurfer.com, finding more information is just a click away.

Index

The images in this book are reproduced through the courtesy of: Henry Wilson, front cover, pp. 7 (left, middle, right), 11, 13(left); Tom & Pat Leeson / Kimballstock, pp. 5, 15; Design Pics Inc / Photolibrary, p. 7 (top), 13 (top); Helmut Meyer zur Capellen / Photolibrary, p. 9; Susan Montgomery, p. 13 (right); David & Micha Sheldon / Photolibrary, p. 17; Herbert Kehrer / Photolibrary, p. 19; Toshiji Fukuda / Minden Pictures, p. 21.

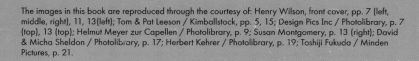